"TIL DEATH DO US PART OR NOT"

"Til Death Do Us Part Or Not"

CJAE JONES

CONTENTS

One	The Day We Met	1
Two	I Do	3
Three	First Year The Hardest	5
Four	The Other Man	7
Five	The Confrontation	9
Six	The Unthinkable	11
Seven	To Death Do Us Part...Right?	14

| one |

The Day We Met

Day started as any normal morning in Washington, DC for these two young adults who started the day as strangers. Kevin woke up to the sound of his alarm blaring. He reached over to silence it, rubbing his eyes as he sat up in bed. Tiffany, already awake, sitting on the edge of her bed reading a book. With a smile, not a normal smile, but the kind that seemed to carry the weight of unspoken things. As Kevin pulled himself out of bed and into the kitchen to prepare breakfast, the rhythmic crackling of eggs on the stove blending with the hum of the city outside. His phone rang, snapping him out of his thoughts.

"Yo, top of the morning, my boy, "Kevin said, answering.

"What's up bro? You headed to the studio yet? Dre's voice crackled through the phone.

"Not yet, man. I'm about to eat something first. Why, What's up?" Kevin responded.

Dre's laughter came through loud and clear. "We're having a kick back at the crib tonight, you left me hanging last time. You are coming through?"

Kevin chuckled, I'm there. Tell them the Spades King is coming through." "Bet, I'll Catch you later bro." Dre hung up

Into the afternoon, Tiffany Leaving brunch with her friends. Realize a familiar face of Rashard, a blast from her past, walked in. They exchanged a surprised greeting, followed by a quick hug.

"You still doing your music thing?" She asked him as they caught up.

"Yeah, I'm still at it. Got a listening party coming up. You should come by, "Rashard suggested, his eyes glinting with something that wasn't just nostalgia. Tiffany hesitated, but the playful flirtation in his voice stirred something deep inside her.

As the evening rolled in, Kevin met Dre at the party, joining a lively crowd of friends, laughter, and card games. He noticed Tiffany, her laughter filling the air as she bantered back and forth with Shayla. So, when the game shifted to something more competitive, Kevin, ever the charmer, laid down a challenge.

"If you win, I'll buy the shots," Tiffany teased, but Kevin only smiled.

"I'm betting something else," he said confidently. "If I win, I want a date." The group went silent, all eyes turning to Tiffany, who laughed, incredulous. "Is that how you ask for a date?"

"Why go small when I'm aiming for the prize?" Kevin shot Back, his voice smooth, his confidence unwavering.

After a round of laughs and challenges, the cards were played, and Tiffany found herself caught in the excitement of that bet, the connection they had rediscovered sparking again. "Alright," she said, a playful glint in her eye, "it's a date."

| two |

I Do

A year passed in what felt like a blink of an eye and now the day has come, their wedding day. A small, intimate ceremony by the beach, the soft waves crashing against the shore as Kevin stood at the altar, his heart pounding with anticipation. Tiffany walked towards him, her smile radiating love and happiness. Their eyes locked, and everything else seemed to fade away.

The Reverend stood between them, a calm presence in the whirlwind of emotions.

"We are gathered here today to witness the union of these two souls in the sight of God," Reverend Adams began, his voice steady. "You both have written your own vows, and now is the time to share them."

Kevin's voice trembled slightly as he spoke, but his words were full of sincerity. "Tiffany, this past year you've been my superwoman, my rock, my best friend. You've been such a blessing to me. And all this started from a card game, from this day forth, I have my forever Spades partner. I Promise to honor and protect you, to grow into the man you encourage me to be, thank you for being my all. I will always fight for us, til death do us part."

Tiffany's eyes glistened with emotion as she spoke, her voice soft but strong. "Kevin, you've been a man of your word, a man of God, and my best friend. I never imagined that a bet over cards would lead me here, but here we are, standing together. I promise to honor and cherish you, to grow with you, and to love you through everything, good times and bad. You are my King, and I am your forever your passenger princess."

The rings were exchanged, and with each word of the ceremony, the weight of their vows settled in deeper. They had chosen each other, and nothing, not the doubts, not the challenges, could take that away. As the Reverend declared them husband and wife, they kissed, and their friends erupted into applause, celebrating the union of two souls who had fought for each other.

| three |

First Year The Hardest

By the time their one-year anniversary arrives, which was only a few weeks away, Kevin had already started to sense the distance between him and his wife. Tiffany was quieter than usual, more distant. She still smiled, laughed, but it wasn't the same. He seen it before, but never like this. The spark they had once shared seemed to be fizzling out, and the harder Kevin tried to reignite it, the more it seemed to slip away.

Even the therapist's office felt colder than Kevin and Tiffany apartment. They sat across from Dr. Tina Moore, their faces tight with tension. The distance between them was palpable, a silent divide neither of them seemed willing to cross.

"It's been a while since our last session. I gave you both an assignment to be more present to your partner. How has that been going?" Dr. Moore asked, her voice calm and probing. Kevin sighed, his gaze dropping to his hands. "I guess you could say I'm here. I'm present... but it's not like it used to be. I don't feel like I'm with my wife anymore." Tiffany, too, looked down, her voice quieter than usual. "We have dinner together. We talk... sometimes. But it feels like I'm just going through the motions."

The doctor nodded, her gaze softening. "It's not uncommon for couples to hit a rough patch, especially in the first year. But it's also a chance to dig deeper, to really listen to each other's needs Kevin,

Tiffany, how can you both start to rebuild what's been lost?" The silence between them lingered. Tiffany, who had always been outgoing, now seemed withdrawn. Kevin's words were tinged with frustration, but he remained committed, determined, at least for now, to make it work.

That anniversary morning, as Kevin watched Tiffany get ready for work, something in his gut knew that this anniversary wasn't going to be like the last one. He bought her a beautiful necklace, hoping it would bring back that sense of excitement, that feeling of being in love. But when he handed it to her, her smile didn't quite reach her eyes.

"Thank you." She said softly. Running her fingers over the delicate chain. "It's beautiful." But Kevin noticed the way her fingers trembled, the way her gaze darted away from him. She wasn't happy. Not in the way she used to be.

| four |

The Other Man

Weeks Passed, and though they tried to reignite the spark they once had, the secrets in their marriage slowly start to creep its way out into the open. Tiffany found reconnecting with someone from her past while trying to figure out her feelings for Kevin, Rashard became more persistent, more present in her life. Not sure how it happened, how she let herself slip into this place of uncertainty. But she couldn't deny the attraction for Rashard. He had always been there, an old flame, a lingering possibility. It felt different. Now, feels like something more.

Started out as something so innocent. A drink here, a text there. Casual meetings cloaked as "old friends just catching up." But the more they saw each other, the more Tiffany realized that Rashard made her feel something she hadn't felt in a long time and that's where everything started to fall apart.

The truth is, Tiffany wasn't sure what she wanted anymore. She loved Kevin, she did, but somewhere this past year she lost herself. So, when she is with Rashard, she feels like her old self, the carefree, fun-loving woman who once was full of life. But she couldn't have both. As months went on, the guilt began to eat at her. She couldn't continue holding this from Kevin, but facing the truth was easier said than done.

But Kevin, too, was fighting his own demons. He buried himself in his work, staying late at the studio, ignoring the growing sense of distance between them. After another long session at the studio, Kevin returned home to find Tiffany gone and with her absence he was reminded of what is missing.

Kevin the next morning pacing back and forth seeming real troubling. He kept pretending everything was fine, but it wasn't.

He spent the last few weeks trying to piece things together, trying to find words that would fix everything, but nothing was working. Tiffany was slipping further away from him, and he finally figured out why.

Tiffany coming out the bedroom. The air was thick with tension as they stood in the living room, facing each other. Tiffany's eyes were red, like she been crying.

"Kevin." she called out

"Tiffany, I already know" Kevin said in his low but firm voice he repeated. "I already know."

| five |

The Confrontation

"Is this who I think it is?" Kevin asked, holding her phone up, the screen flashing with messages from Rashard. "How long has this been going on, Tiffany?

Tiffany froze, looking like a deer caught in headlights. The truth was out, and now it was time to face it.

"How long?" Kevin's voice fill with pain and hurt. Even though he asked, deep down he didn't want to know the truth

Tiffany bit her lip, taking a deep breath. "It been a while now."

But at this point Kevin wasn't paying no attention, the hurt of hearing the truth was too much. The betrayal cut too deep. He couldn't look at her the same anymore. The woman he chose to marry was gone, replaced by someone else who didn't belong to him. Turning his back to her to try to hide the pain that started to show on his face.

Tiffany eyes filled with guilt, could barely find the words to explain as she reaches out for him. "Kevin, please, let me explain," she pleaded

"Explain what? How you've been with another man?" Kevin's voice cracked with pain and anger, each word spoken heavier than the last. "You've been sleeping with him all this time, behind my back, how could you do that to me?"

Kevin, at his lowest, spiraled into deep internal struggle, questioning his worth, his ability to love. But despite all the turmoil, Tiffany was determined to make amends. She still loved him, and she wasn't ready to let go, not without trying everything to repair what had been broken. The place that once was filled with laughter, love, and dreams now felt cold, sterile. He'd thought he could fix it, thought he could make everything right. But now it felt like there was no way back. His heart was fill with anger, heartbreak, and numbness. He couldn't feel anymore. Not the way he used to.

| six |

The Unthinkable

Seeing the hurt and pain on Kevin's Face. Tiffany, walked in the room face pale, her eyes blood shot red from crying. She apologizes again "I'm sorry, Kevin," she whispered, her voice hoarse.

Kevin looked at her with a blank stare, words and thoughts running in his head but none of them seemed to help ease the hurt. He had so much anger and pain. But there was something deeper, something dark, something he couldn't control.

Sorry, Sorry just don't cut it for me anymore. You're sorry?" His voice cracked, and the tears he had been fighting off finally starting flowing.

Tiffany took a step to him reaching out, but Kevin recoiled, his chest tightening. He couldn't breathe. "Don't touch me." He responded

I didn't want this to happen," Tiffany said, tears pouring down her face. "But I was lost, Kevin. I don't know who I am anymore

Kevin laughed bitterly, the sound foreign and hollow. "So fucking another dude was the answer huh? Not counseling? But Cheating?" He shook his head. "Now you expect me to forgive you? I loved you. I gave you everything in me."

Tiffany wanted to say something but every time she opened her mouth, the words wouldn't come out. All she had left was apologies, but they were empty. She couldn't take back what was already done.

Kevin turned away, He couldn't take it anymore. He couldn't be the man who let this go. He was spiraling, and he knew it, but he didn't care at this point. There was only one way to make the pain stop. He walked to the bedroom, his mind a blur of rage and disbelief. Tiffany followed but when he opened the lockbox from under the bed, her eyes widened in shock.

No, Kevin. Please," she said with her voice sounding desperate.

Kevin pulled out the gun, hands shaking. To him there's no turning back now. He couldn't face the world anymore. The betrayal, the lies. He felt like he was losing himself, like there was nothing left to fight for.

Kevin, no!" Tiffany screamed, running toward him. But he was already beyond the point of return. Tiffany's breath hitched as she lunged at him, trying to take the gun from his hands. In that moment, with the pressure of everything. The hurt, the pain, the uncertainty was too much. Kevin pulled the trigger

The sound of the gunshot echoed in the room. Tiffany stood frozen, her heart racing, her mind spinning. The man she loved, the man who given her everything, was now a stranger. Staring at the blood on the floor, the gun lying next to her. Kevin collapsed right beside her, his chest rising and falling weakly. She could hardly breathe; her body numb still in shock. Everything had happened too fast.

She tried to stop him. She tried to save him she keeps telling herself. But now, all she could do was sit there in the wreckage unable to make sense of anything that happen.

Kevin's eyes fluttered open, his breath ragged. But he didn't speak. His gaze was distant, unfocused. Tiffany's heart broke all over again. He had always been her rock. Her support. But now, she was the one who had broken them. Even worst broken him, she failed him.

Kevin..." she whispered, reaching out to touch his hand. The hand that once felt warm and soft now feel firm and cold.

| seven |

To Death Do Us Part...Right?

Six months later, It's Kevin's birthday, but there was no celebration. Instead, Tiffany visiting his grave. A single tear fell as she knelt beside his headstone, her heart still heavy with sorrow.

To my forever love." she whispered, holding a bouquet of balloons. "I miss you so much. I know I messed up. But I'm going to make things right, not just for you, but for our son. Yes, you hear that baby? We're having a boy. I'll make sure he knows you, Kevin. He will know you were loved and the best man I ever knew.

"Til death do us part," Kevin had once said to her, in their vows. But Tiffany knew now that it wasn't just about surviving to the end. It was about choosing each other, every day. The air around her seemed to still, the weight of the past year pressing down on her, she let it all go releasing the balloons into the sky, hoping that somehow, wherever he was he could hear her.

The silence of the cemetery weighed heavily on Tiffany as she stood there, staring at Kevin's headstone. The cold wind brushed against her face, but she barely noticed. Everything around her seemed distant, like the world was moving on while she remained frozen in time. The memory of their love, the laughter, the vows, and the heartbreak, all swirled together like a dream she could never fully wake up from. Her hands trembled as she touched the cold stone, her fingers tracing his name as if she could somehow feel his presence.

"I'm so sorry, Kevin," she whispered. "I should have been better. I should have done better.

The tears flowed freely now, her heart aching in a way she couldn't explain. She'd tried to move on to rebuild her life, but some things could never be fixed. And then, in the quiet. She closed her eyes, her lips trembling. She made one final vow.

"To death do us part.... right?"

www.ingramcontent.com/pod-product-compliance
Lightning Source LLC
LaVergne TN
LVHW051927060526
838201LV00062B/4717